ASK ME

Fay Zwicky was born in Melbourne in 1933. She began writing as an undergraduate at the University of Melbourne. Formerly a concert pianist, she taught Literature at the University of Western Australia until retirement in 1987. Her first collection of short stories, *Hostages*, was published in 1983. This is the third collection of her poetry following *Isaac Babel's Fiddle* (1975) and *Kaddish and Other Poems* (1982) which won the NSW Premier's Award.

By the same author:

Poetry
Isaac Babel's Fiddle
Kaddish and Other Poems

Short Stories
Hostages

Essays
The Lyre in the Pawnshop

As editor
Quarry
Journeys
Procession

ASK ME

FAY ZWICKY

University of Queensland Press

First published 1990 by University of Queensland Press
Box 42, St Lucia, Queensland 4067 Australia

© Fay Zwicky 1990

This book is copyright. Apart from any fair dealing
for the purposes of private study, research, criticism
or review, as permitted under the Copyright Act, no
part may be reproduced by any process without written
permission. Enquiries should be made to the publisher.

Typeset by University of Queensland Press
Printed in Australia by Australian Print Group, Maryborough,
Victoria

Distributed in the USA and Canada by
International Specialized Book Services, Inc.,
5602 N.E. Hassalo Street, Portland, Oregon 97213-3640

Creative writing program assisted
by the Literature Board of the
Australia Council, the Federal Government's
arts funding and advisory body

Cataloguing in Publication Data

National Library of Australia

Zwicky, Fay, 1933-
  Ask me.

  I. Title.

A821.3

ISBN 0 7022 2282 8

For J.A.C.M.
who did.

Acknowledgments

Australian Broadcasting Company, Fathers and Writers Programme: "Afloat"
The *Florida Review,* USA: "Father in a Mirror", "Southern Spell", "Jack Frost in Florida", "Band Music for a Grandfather"
Helix: "A Tale of the Great Smokies", "The Ballad of the Pretty Young Wife"
Island Magazine: "Soup and Jelly", "Breathing Exercises"
Meanjin: "In Memory, Vincent Buckley 1925-1988", "Devi"
Northern Perspective: "Jacques Tati at the Darwin Hotel"
Overland: "Afloat", "Broadway Vision", "The Temple: Ganesh", "Siva" (under the title "Siva Dancing")
Peterloo Poets, UK, *Poetry Matters* and *Causley at 70:* "The Call"
Phoenix Review: "For A.D. Hope", "Marius in Hobart, 1989"
Quadrant: "Miss Short Instructs Her Latin Class . . .", "Pie in the Sky"
The *Raddle Moon,* Canada: "Vishnu"
Southerly: "Reading"
The *Weekend Australian:* "Over the Wall", "Passing", "Tiananmen Square, June 4, 1989"
Westerly: "For Jim, 1947-1986"

Contents

I

China Poems 1988
- I   *Roosters and Earthworms*   3
- II   *Out of this World*   5
- III   *Over the Wall*   8
- IV   *Passing*   10
- *Tiananmen Square, June 4, 1989*   11

The Temple, Somnapura
- I   *Ganesh*   13
- II   *Vishnu*   17
- III   *Siva*   20
- IV   *Devi*   23

Four Poems from America
- I   *Father in a Mirror*   28
- II   *Southern Spell*   29
- III   *Jack Frost in Florida*   30
- IV   *Band Music for a Grandfather*   31

A Tale of the Great Smokies
- 1   *Otis Makes a Wheel*   32
- 2   *Penelope Spins*   34
- 3   *Uriah Mack behind the Sassafras*   36
- 4   *Otis Raises Sheep*   38
- 5   *Penelope and the Lambs*   41
- 6   *Uriah is Hired by Otis*   44
- 7   *The Shearing*   46
- 8   *The Dyeing*   48

II

Broadway Vision   *53*
The Call   *57*
Pie in the Sky   *59*
For A.D. Hope   *63*
Growing Up   *65*
Reading a Letter in Amsterdam   *66*
The Ballad of the Pretty Young Wife   *68*
Jacques Tati at the Darwin Hotel   *71*
Marius in Hobart, 1989   *73*
New Age   *76*
Miss Short Instructs Her Latin Class on the Fountains of Nepenthe, 1912   *77*

III

Hospice Training   *83*
Breathing Exercises   *85*
Afloat   *86*
Call It Love   *87*
Reading   *88*
Home Care   *90*
Soup and Jelly   *94*
In Memory, Vincent Buckley 1925-1988   *96*
For Jim 1947-1986   *99*

Notes   *106*

I

China Poems 1988

I Roosters and Earthworms

It's the year of the Dragon.
Omens for the journey aren't encouraging.
No language and I'm booked
on China Airlines. In Hong Kong I dream
that I am born without a tongue
and wake up screaming . . .

I'm studying the twelve animal signs.
Or did the Revolution do away with them?
Too frivolous maybe? The Irish in me
thinks there may be something in it
all the same. Keep reading –

Are you a sentimental but crafty Rat?
A dutiful Ox?
A smashing but unpredictable Tiger?
I am a Rooster.
Honest, frank, obliging, difficult
to live with.
Spot on, so far. What's this?
Vain? Despotic? Prickly about criticism?
Perhaps there's nothing in it
after all.

Tradition has it that I'd find
an earthworm in the desert.

My best roles are military hero or clown.
Not much to choose between them but
I'll settle for the latter, never liked
the army much (the Irish rises up again),
my worst is spy – I'm too conspicuous.

Roosters don't mean to hurt your feelings.
They simply like to let you know
your food's inedible, your hygiene's foul,
your creature comforts nil, you're vain,
despotic, prickly about criticism.

Rooster celebrities include:
Catherine the Great, Colette, Copernicus
and Kierkegaard (the company's not improving),
Marie de Medici, Strindberg, Queen Victoria
and, wouldn't you know, Wagner.

I'd better watch myself.
Plenty of other roosters on the farm.
Earthworms never grew on trees.
This is where it all began.

II Out of this World

I'm in Beijing.
When I was young it was Peking.
Fans and silk and lacquered screens,
sages playing chess in elegant pavilions
on the Flowery Mountain . . .

It's minus 4.
The heating system thumped all night,
the cistern trickled.
At school we called it Chinese Torture,
gave each other Chinese Burns.
China was a name to conjure with
when we were young, light-years away,
out of this world.

It's 5.30 A.M. and I've been downstairs twice.
Nobody there.

Down in a vast reading room for students
I saw two dogeared journals, *China Reconstructs,*
in a bookcase with glass doors.
Not a book in sight.
Someone left a Chinese newspaper.
I can't read a word. Who am I here?

The water taps are dry.
The colours in my room bring back
Australian holidays, dead brown grainless
pub wardrobes, kitchen-green walls,
dun green felt carpeting.
Under the bed with its embroidered pillowslip
lie two used plastic scuffs. They're also green.
There's a tall red anodised thermos
flanked by two sachets of coarse tea-leaves,
rough as bonsai'd mallee roots. Two mugs with lids.

Something square stands sheathed in black.
Velvet and sinister, it's in a corner.
I lift a flap. A TV set, the antenna's
a Chinese character inside a hoop of steel.
Two diabolic little horns point upward.
Many knobs, a cord, no powerpoint.
I lift the phone.
It buzzes like a thousand swarming bees.
I put it down.

Don't look out the window yet.
Try to deal with what's inside.

At 6 the water starts.
My bath looks like the Red River.
I slumber in the river, part of me
awake on CA Flight 309, marking
before the symptom "if any now"
Fever   Rash   Cough
Bleeding   Psychosis   Leprosy
Aids
I've got them all.

The river's still,
becalmed above red sediment.

Below the window on a concrete path
a man in black stands motionless.
Black gloves, black coat, a cap.
Is he really standing there
below my bathroom window?
I look hard again holding my breath.
He's there all right.

He's all alone.
The dawn is rising red before him.
He doesn't know or care
that there's a frightened watcher
following his stillness like a dream.

But he's turning slowly now   slowly
like a dream he turns and folds his hands
as if in slowest prayer
first one side and then slowly
to the other, light-years away
and out of this world.

He isn't young.

III Over the Wall

Today we go to the Wall.
The sun shines, the bus is small.

We loose Australians pile obediently in.
We laugh moderately.
One of us is making a joke.
We can't go overboard here.

Later we'll go over the top
of the Wall. When we get out.

Our two guardians sit up straight
in Mao jackets up the front,
between them a neat pile of paper bags.
Our playlunch.

We're diplomatic and attentive.
I hardly recognise us.

Far down the back sit students.
They are quiet and gentle.
They don't go overboard either.
They may not get out
until the visitors have left.

The sun shines on.
We climb the Wall.
The magic mountains better all our dreams,
their peaks razored against
an endless sky.

Clearly their painters invented nothing.
Looked and recorded
looked and recorded the changeless
whetstoned cones with maybe a man
somewhere down in a corner,
very small and very wise.

We climb and look again.
The eye oscilloscopes along and back
along and back . . .

A student carrying my bag is watching me.
She smiles. "You like it here?"
How can I tell her that
I'm neither happy nor unhappy?

How can I tell her that I've seen
a man at the foot of these ageless peaks
a man who has turned away,
a man who is very small and very wise?

She might think I was seeing things.

IV Passing

Dreams are the suicides of the well-behaved.

Do the Chinese have great and wonderful powers
of forgetfulness?
Or do they dream like anybody else?

I met a man living in the same building
as the man who killed his father.

He refused to take the lift
in case he met this man.

He walks up six flights of stairs twice a day.
The lift passes up and down slowly
and he watches the iron cage pass.

I dream a poor boy's dream of China,
the story of silence.
The men who pass his father's grave each day,
and walking, raise their caps slowly
without speaking.

Tiananmen Square
June 4, 1989

Karl Marx, take your time,
looming over Highgate on your plinth.
Snow's falling on your beard,
exiled, huge, hairy, genderless.
Terminally angry, piss-poor,
stuffed on utopias and cold,
cold as iron.

I'm thinking of your loving wife,
your desperate children and your grandchild
dead behind the barred enclosure of your brain.
Men's ideas the product, not the cause
of history, you said?

The snow has killed the lilacs.
Whose idea?
The air is frozen with theory.

What can the man be doing all day
in that cold place?
What can he be writing?
What can he be reading?
What big eyes you have, mama!
Next year, child, we will eat.

I'm thinking of my middle-class German grandmother
soft as a pigeon, who wept
when Chamberlain declared a war.
Why are you crying, grandma?
It's only the big bad wolf, my dear.
It's only a story.

There's no end to it.
The wolves have come again.
What shall I tell my grandchildren?

No end to the requiems, the burning trains,
the guns, the shouting in the streets,
the outraged stars, the anguished face
of terror under ragged headbands
soaked in death's calligraphy.

Don't turn your back, I'll say.
Look hard.
Move into that frozen swarming screen.
How far can you run with a bullet in your brain?

And forgive, if you can, the safety of a poem
sharpened on a grieving night.

A story has to start somewhere.

The Temple, Somnapura

*Choose for your Stone him through whom
kings are honoured in their crowns,
and through whom physicians heal their
sick, for he is near to the fire.*
              Rosarium philosophorum (1550)

I Ganesh

Footfall
smooth   cool
soothing the sole
arched and released
soundless in
underworld spaces

tread inward
down and
down   slow
slow
lightening the arch
press   swaying on
smoothness on
oiled pilgrimed
soles softened
to yearning
stone
down

Footfall
released arch
loosed to the
edge
the edge

and down
inward
inward —

Faith is the sound
of a man breathing
alone in darkness
emptied

Faith is his patience
tenure on foot-fastened
stone
prayer to an
absence

To learn the Emptiness of the bare mind
Without knowledge . . .

Is truth so smooth
so bald
so stark
so dumb as temple stone?

A light shaft strikes the stone,
mints spry slumped corpulent Ganesh,
elephant-crowned runt
of jealous Siva,
the enormous first parent —

Grant, O Lord, we beseech Thee
won't do here —

Affliction fathers gods and men,
our first shame equal.

Ganesh leans his ponderous bulk
upon the open world, his trunk
ripples with laughter.

Pad slow   slow
moulding the foot
to the swell and the fall
the cool stone
breathing —

Echoes swirl the ancient ceiling
voices   voices
cries in little flames lick
sacred texts in smoke
half-caught forms
bells   incense
        dung

Light the tall bronze lamps.
Feed them oil.
Twist the wicks to flicker
over blue-black hair —

Siva's eye beheads his son
and there he sits, docked,
bowed in elephantine sorrow.

Even gods may be ambiguous,
hate their wives,
their children.

His hands fold slyly in prayer,
lips part like shells
to whispering waves of stone —

Women kneel in pious shadows
tracing sinuous whorls of coloured flour,
wisped by incense.
Blue-black oiled hair, white gleaming
cluster upon cluster climb,
trembling jasmine, nightshade, marigolds
garlands of orange   green   gold —

Astride a bandicoot
lord Ganesh laughs.
A short fat marvellous child
bulbous bright, four arms
blistered with bees
three eyes behind his
rippling trunk —

Slumbering in stone
he leans upon the whispers of the dark,
night's nursery.
His fine molested grace remembers
promises of love
towards his difference:

Indra's goad
Padmavati's lotus
coloured inks from Sarasvati
a tiger skin from father Siva
a sacrificial thread from
roaring Brihaspati.
And from the goddess Earth, a rat
to draw his stunting chariot.

Becalmed in stone
his lotus face smiles down
amused and absent —

Retreating from the light
of his now-fathering force,
our human shadows print us small
like crippled children.

II *Vishnu*

No precepts here
but slow unravellings –

>   Vish
>   nu
>   Kri
>   shn
> avish
>   nu
>   Krish
>   na
>   a a a a

pitched against the One
the One forever changeless God
who swaddles mutinous children's hands
and stops their mouth –

The body and the soul know how to play
In that dark world where gods have lost their way.

Light air and silence kiss
the lazy lotus lip.
Vishnu, rapt in fleshless sleep
under his curly crown,
once tumultuous

The sun, a scorching nectarine
rolls aside the misty scarves
wreathing the violet blur of
distant hills. Green hosts of parakeets
all shriek and blaze and dazzle
divine the coming of the god. Morning quickens,
mounts. All moves and sways suspended.

Tilting crows cut ever-widening circles high
above the creaking sway of carts
a steady bullock chomp of straw.
Well-wheels grinding   grinding grinding
tiny matchstick forms dot out
the hazy wakening fields,
the long slow hum of breathless morning.

Pensive wives of cowherds toss
on tousled beds.
Come, lord Krishna, hear their song:

> "My pillow won't tell me
> Where he has gone,
> The soft-footed one
> Who passed by, alone.
>
> Who took my heart whole,
> With a tilt of his eye,
> And with it, my soul,
> And it like to die."

Our lord with lotus eyes
has raised a mountain.
Dark as storm his blue-black wings
lift all of us dark stragglers
to glory.
        Spending his force
against soft-bellied rush of musk,
dark turns fair, rain turns fire,
forms dissolve in music.

Balm to fissured earth, he shimmers
to his flute, filling the fervid lips
the thighs that spin like bowls
upon a potter's wheel.
Such tricks and turns take milkmaid,
cowherd, flowergirl, goddess all as one
while tender-stepping herons sit and
strut and rock the limpid waters by
the cunning groves of Vrinavan.

The pleasure lakes brim white with lilies
aloes saffron sandalwood when Krishna,
sleek as an otter, teases his way.
His love drives headlong like a spear
through a green tree.
The pliant women swell and fret and foam
like indolent water weeds on stormy seas.
"Tell us your name" they beg,
trying to recall his face —

Vishnu naps and multiplies.
He has a million million years to go.

Lord of the wheel has shattered shame
in myriad shapes.

He smiles to think how once
a slippery blue-black boy leaped out of swaddling
into sunlight, becoming fish, wild boar, a million
magic shapes . . .

Silence flowers on his lips.
The temple garlands wink in candlelight,
their musky clusters soaring to
a solitary half-heard flute.

III Siva

Though dancing needs a master, I had none
To teach my toes to listen to my tongue.
But what I learned there, dancing all alone,
Was not the joyless motion of a stone.
               Theodore Roethke, "The Dance"

  God-step

Upraised palm

    phat!

two subtle fingers
seeking upper air
and up the high-
curved thigh —

Stone stirs to circling music

cobra shoulder snaking
           round
                  and
    down
        the arm flows
      down a
            length to fine-
      point
   fingers
         down
  and
     down to
   tapered limb
    to
   rooted
   foot

Eternal joy outleaps the
flame-spoked wheel.

Tongue lags and leaden lies
before the lightning miracle of dance.

Healthy and terrible, Siva sifts his memories
like rolling sesame seeds and dancing, sings
a song of hearty tyranny:

"My voice rolls out in thunder claps
forked the lightning of my weapon's flash,
cuts zigzag paths for my far-seeing,
my tongue a breaking wave.

I grind the earth — it rocks.
I rend the earth — it quakes.
Firm as the earth's axis is
my high-arched foot —

it tumbles the mountain buffalo
pounds burial grounds
topples garden coconuts splits
figs like peas —"

Such childish rages!

Ah, they said, *but children only
curl their lotus toes and stamp unseasoned
lie and sprawl exhausted.*
                Siva knows
what secrets curve a foot
the weight   the measure
height and depth of planting.
Let him sing out his season:

"I land like a vulture on rocks.
My eye sinks sun and moon
the hooded snake my eyelid,
my slinking tiger-shadow lurks, my mount
a gravid elephant."

New shapes for old! New shapes for old!

"Like dreaming moon in water   or mirage
on the wide spring plain,
nothing is changeless.

Going I stay
Staying I go

My anklets clash I
raise and curve my left haunch
high   higher   higher
    above   the
       rooted
        foot
           and ever round
    the fiery wheel
      turning   turning
        turning."

Dusky powdered human forms
flit shadow-black, blue sapphire-
faceted in fitful spurts of
candleflame
Smoking censers swinging golden
chains linking tiny tinkling bells
surging swinging silken saris
jewelpoints sandalwood   sheen of
musk-oiled hair merging into
      light   stone
        silence

IV Devi

Only Siva, meditating,
could be immovable
in her moving presence.

Tread slow   slower
inward and down
soften the loosened
arch lower
lower   heavily
down
downward to
smooth softened
sole   rising
falling
breathing in
darkness
down –

Ganesha's mother
mother of life
mother of death
sealed in man's
misgivings –

she sanctifies the morning
with her sightless eyes
calm   unhaunted

broad rounded haunches
breasts and melon-swollen
belly, heavy thighs
a massive fruitful
cluster . . .

What sways the soul
is what's invisible.

Light breaks bronzed
over these fecund rounds
flexing around the fluid
girlish waist, curving up
and around, so slender
leaflike chaste, mocking
the dense exuberance
below.

Once a girl, a green thing
quickening, she couldn't guess
beyond the clutch of wind
and flame the rising
falling spiral, bud to
fruit to bursting
back to aching blackness
of infirmity to
ashes, compost.

Once a girl, she sang
without a mouth, high
on a granite mountain —

a floating tenderness
brief as twilight

upraised tendril arms
swaying hips and silver
circling anklets rounding
slender legs drawn
down by beauty's
weight to
earth.

Her water pot of bronze
shining in the setting sun
plumbed wells of deep content,
her parents' borderless kingdom.

Days fell silently like leaves.
Words moved slow as glaciers.

But warring gods and demons pushed
to woo night's daughter,
monster-husbands.

Her bowels turned brass and iron
breasts burst with bitter milk
the rocking thighs imparting
shape   pitch   weight to mouth
agape —
her eyes drained sorrow's
salty marshes.

O gentle angry mother,
girl that man knows nothing of,
stretched high on a volcano's rim
voicing the tribe's cruel energies:

a meditating head from Siva
arms from Vishnu's vigorous fires
from Brahma's thighs the passionate feet
from Indra's serpent shape a gliding waist
the brush-fire of her hair from Yama
breasts from the ardent moon
thighs from forked Varuna, all-enveloping
god of waters   ears shelled from
the wind's streaming   teeth   white
as curd from the nine Prajapatis
under a sullen twilight brow
eyes fish-pools deepening
into oblation.

Ample water jar
bath of birth   vessel of death
       grain-giver

Lady of milky rain
brooks   streams   fountains
indifferent —

Lady of scorpions   serpents
goose   crowned heron   quail
indifferent —

Lady of bull   goat   wolf   deer
hunting and hunted
indifferent —

griffin   phoenix   sphinx
indifferent —

Lady of caves   tombs   skulls
indifferent —

Gods and men have mothers.
We are her infants slumbering
like sleepy planets
circling endless whiteness —

We suck and turn and
hide our faces.

Footfall

sightless   all-seeing
godhead   cobra-smiling

absence

a lotus opens,
suppliant in
sunlight —

Four Poems from America

I Father in a Mirror

In the morning mirror
you are here in me my eyes
surprised as from our bitter Sundays
cautious, hopeful
silent.

You said, *If it weren't for the Americans* . . .
while I fought on the other side,
a sullen parody of independence
back in '46.

But Dad, you're here and
I'm the parent now, the shy
explorer taking care and looking
for you at you
in America.

II *Southern Spell*

The Apopka Blue Darters are coming to play
coming to play, coming to play
by Lake Osceola in spring –

Aloisus and Shad
Sylvie and Tad
Nancie and Tabitha and Quinton and Ziggy
Archello, Idalia, Rocco and Lili
Fleetwood, Cecilia, Wink and Clarissa
Dessie and Ulmo, Tibor and Jitter
Zippa, la Donna, Hub, Thane and Rusty
scamper and nibble by Lake Osceola.

The Apopka Blue Darters are coming to play
The town intellectuals have all run away.

It's a great day!

III Jack Frost in Florida

An unexpected place to take his ease.
Will it appease his slow fatigue?

His eyes ablaze with
Oranges   Oranges
more
a hundred
thousand burning in the tracings
of his hourless breath.

He glides upon them
like a storm
clamping their fires out
one by one

his cloaking dream furls
fouls a green-gold world
to brown to
black to

sleep, Jack, sleep.
World, button your coat tight.
Black is white.

IV Band Music for a Grandfather

Why should I fear death today?
My daughter is tooting her bass clarinet
in a real American band.

the high school band
the high school band
the neatest band in this jumping land.
She plays with Chuck and Dwight and Wayne
Elvira and Jimmy and Toby and Jane
and O America salves the pain
as the music soars and roars in the rain.

The space shuttle's up and my spirit's away.
O say can you hear your little one play?
Say, should I fear old death today?
O say

A Tale of the Great Smokies

1 Otis Makes a Wheel

*I have neither the looks nor the
stature of the immortal gods but
am a human being.*

Any kind of hard wood will do, she said
but soon, make it soon.

So I made wheel and hub,
bench and head post of white pine,
spokes of cherry.
The front leg cut from our white poplar
by the well, back legs of maple.

I turned the rounds on a water-lathe,
driven by the stream behind our house,
even with my axe hacked out the dovetail
notch that her thread might
lie easy.

I split the rims from one straight
green white oak and thought my arms
would break. She soothed and urged.
Each day I brought a little of myself
for her approval.

Each end was tapered,
and I drew the split into a circle,
caught the ends together with some pegs.
Then set the wheel up in the attic,
pressed out flat so not to warp it
out of round while curing.

Soon enough, I said, these things
can't hurry.
Like me she'll come to live with limits
Like me she'll learn what can't be taught.

Somewhere beyond all this drift
the stars are reckoning us up.

2 Penelope Spins

and there she wept for Odysseus

Turn from the word
turn away, he said, schooled in silence.
Made a true wheel, then easy
as breathing, moved down the river
poling his skiff into mist.
                                    Thin neck
stiffening, set up to catch the winds of this world
in the long hot shaft of our dying summer.

Loving too much, not enough maybe, hardly a
seeker but cheerful. He had his illusions –
we were one of them.
Things went much as usual.
Maybe the stars had a hand in it,
or the one fixed star of my own
grim seeking whose light
blurs my sight like a
drunkard's candle.

Tread air, tread light
silent as dust riding darkness.
Treadle and turn,
black bobbin fat in my fingers.

Soft as moth's breath,
threads slip through tides of my handling,
wordless to wait on his coming,
fixed in my longing for speech.

Compost   black currant
fodder   horse urine
hickory   smoke
           Breath lives,
wavers within.
              Far below, wide
over the valley burn farmlights
through fog. Dusty signals from
neighbouring hearths.

Tread air, tread light
silent as sleepers in darkness
treadle and turn, unlearn
the bulk of our being, unwind
the tight bobbin. Stand
naked as two spindles saying
in one deep-drawn breath
"I am."

Tread air, tread light
turn again, little wheel.
Darkness has secrets that
light never owns.

3 Uriah Mack behind the Sassafras

It's either a goddess or a woman.

She doesn't see me. My pulse is a trout
in my wrist.
                The hen tails her string
of yellow chicks with alarm to the barn.

She sleeps in herself like a stone
in the sun, shaping the threads
of his going.

She sings to the air, winding,
unwinding the threads:
"Turn again, turn again
little wheel ever.
He shall have what I am
when he crosses the river."

Neat as a bird in her red headscarf,
loose blond-greying hair
sun-bleached eyes scanning water.
A distaff of ripe dark wood
pressed close, under her arm
near her breast. Puffball of
rusty black fleece near her shoulder,
spinning the old way.
                Brown fingers plucking
teasing the strands drawn under
to wind the black bobbin as fast
as the wind.

Still centre of everything, sun-worn
like stone, hands leaping
caressing like drunken butterflies
fretting the shuttle.
                              It snags on a
hickory twig at her foot.
Bending to free it, I move.
She backs off, her eyes an unblinking
promise of instant refusal.

There but unseen, suspended to rock
in the wake of her song, I slouch
through the path of her
passionate waiting, scorpion
under a stone.

A daddy's house is nothing
but a cardboard box.

4 Otis Raises Sheep

*The fruit never fails nor runs
short, winter and summer alike.*

Forty years I tended flocks
on Blue Ridge like my pa before.
We grew the critters just for wool –
a smaller and a hardier strain, no
bigger than your average dog – you
couldn't buy 'em.

Most everybody back
when I was growing up just
kept the ones they wanted.
Stood the cold, the barren times,
never sickened.
Shy and timid too, they ran
in fear from feral beasts,
would let themselves be killed
without a fight. Once caught
and scared, they just gave up.

Most was white but now and then
a black cropped out.
We liked a black born onst
a while. It saved us
from the dyeing.

We shared the extra wool with them
that didn't keep a flock.
Come spring, I fenced the yard and
turned them loose to graze the mountains.
Maybe they'd come back for salt
once a month or so. We didn't take it
to them on account of fearing
that they wouldn't come. You give 'em
salt. Two, three days after they're
gone again.
                    All summer long they'd go
a long ways off and stay.

                    In fall we'd get out,
hunt 'em up and bring 'em down
through winter.

To tell our own, we notched their ears
on top – Uriah Mack, my neighbour
split the whole ear through
to make a swallow-fork.
I knowed it when we swapped a ram
or two to keep from interbreeding.
We had our marks and knew our own,
but shared.
                    Times were the rams would
fight but mostly get along. The
old ones on the mountain had those
long curved horns they'd lock together.
Times were when they'd starve to death
locked in struggle. We found a couple
once, overbit and swallow-fork dusted
with snow, but still we knew the owners.

She wanted to be sure they'd come
down from the mountain in the cold.
I told her often enough they
had to come, just like we do.
                              When they want
a thing or two they come. They
wouldn't hardly if they didn't
find a need.

A home don't need no fences.

If anything gets after them
they know to come.
Like us, they want a place at night
to stay, a barn for heavy snows
fine grasses — blue or tender rye —
blades off cane. And voices.

I tell her every time they all come
back. She's only happy once they're
fastened in the barn and feeding.

5 Penelope and the Lambs

> *the gods had robbed them of their parents,*
> *left them orphaned in their home; and yet*
> *they lived . . .*

Spring was always best,
took hold of me like nothing else.

The land's slopes softened green
and graceful right down to
the valley, downward rolled
the children, shook themselves
like little dogs in dotted
fields of lavender.
      Then lambs would
wobble up to suck their ewes
who sniffed and pawed them
into patience.

The old kind nursed their young,
would hold their jug up for 'em,
push the baby to it — either
take it or you die — was in the
tilt.
   No matter what the cold,
they'd clean their babies, dry them
with their mouths, hold breath
right up against them. I'd catch
the puffs of moist warm air hanging
round the little strugglers
in the chill of morning.

There was an orphan once.
I raised it all the way
till it was grown. Then
took it to the barn. It lived.
That beat most things I've
ever seen.

      It followed me all through
the house and if I'd get away, it
just stood bleating like my children
when I left a room.

If a mother died, he'd shut the lamb
up with another ewe and force
the feeding on a stranger.

We saved a lot between us,
thinking over.

Spring was always best. To yawn and
stretch and look and love it all.
Even the dark edge
of the distant wood.

My thoughts like little pine cones
float in warmth like feathers,
puffs of milkweed

Dogwood's thick white petals
fretsaw clean against the four black cedars
by the well, the tender push of green
by oak and walnut.
It catches at the heart, almost
like a sorrow I might say
if I didn't know it different.

Roses, phlox and pansies cut a fancy apron
round the yellow house, and everywhere
the smell of wood-smoke, dewberries
the river.

Silenced by joy,
the colour, smell and sound
of everything answer
any question I have
ever asked.

Why talk of time, children, spring
and a river if not to tell
that once we spoke and
listened to each other.

6 Uriah is Hired by Otis

Who knows but we may oust him
from the threshold and the door . . .

Help her when I'm gone
like neighbours do, he said.
She'll need the shearing
come spring and maybe
early fall.
                See that the
well don't dry, the house
stays warm. I ain't been parted
but two days from her before.
I'll pay.

The sun was setting like a big red ball
and yes, I said,
it wouldn't give no trouble
helping out.
There ain't a broken thing
I couldn't fix and
where, I said, my mind
a nest of buzzards, would
you find a dreaming woman
like your own?

I guess a body's like a house
he said, thin and even, but
the spirit keeps on moving.
This time, he said, I'm
putting two and two together.

Seems, I said, like putting
two apart. I don't know
about spirits but this body's

staying put. She won't give me
no trouble. She's smart.
I've watched her spin and weave,
no age on her at all. Most
tenant wives are not the kind
you want around for long, but
yours . . . you're more a fool
than what I ever thought.

He went that summer.
I waited out the winter
till she sent her boy to ask
for shearing in the spring.
If he can help me hold 'em down,
I said, it's twenty head a day
or more, taking the measure
of everything. They're small,
remember; nothing much on legs
or tail — it shouldn't take
but six at most.
Maybe, she said. I'll feed you
give you room and pay like
Otis said. Lady, I said, there's
some around that certain things
mean more to them
than money.
          I asked her what she
thought a man was made for.
She never answered. Called the
hen quick into the barn,
her straggle of yellow chicks
behind her.

   "Turn again, turn again
   little wheel ever"

That song again.
Buzzards hatch in spring too.

7 The Shearing

> *He'll have your nose and ears off with*
> *his cruel knife, rip away your parts*
> *and give them raw to dogs.*

The boy was watching sullen
as I held the first upright,
front legs stiffened
in my grasp.

Cut sure and deep around the neck
the head and down along the
heaving belly
down to hind legs limply splayed
the soft crotch twitching
peeled the curling sheath
off one side. One fat layer.

Just like you skin an animal,
the boy said rigid, pale,
standing aside.

Then fastening the head
between my legs, I shaved
in one fast sweep the
back of neck and shoulder
smoothly down the back
to tail, then down
the shivering flank
in one swift rush
of fattened fleece.

It's like you skinned
a rabbit or a bear, he said again
or something else you wanted bad.
That kid.

She came to gather up the fleece
for washing, filled a metal
tub, hot water and lye soap
and scrubbed. Then laid it
out in heavy swatches to dry
on clean rocks by the stream.
Never spoke a word, not even
to the kid who stood aside
sullen, pale.

I took another sheep between my legs.
Its muscles bunched against my hands.

You have to give them time.

8 The Dyeing

*And now, as easily as a musician
who knows his lyre strings . . .*

First threads and last.

Smooth thick pale cow-cud
green darkening through oak
past walnut to the pine wood's
distant rim. By now
I know its darkness.

I have dreamed of water.

His flesh was green, the taut
skin of his neck and every
tendon straining out, his face
white against a cold green wall
of water like the stream that
turned his lathe.
It pulled and sucked
swirled mud beneath our feet.

We were suspended so.
Erect in turn, green currents
curling, dimpling round our
naked shoulders in ever-widening
slow dark whorls.

Suddenly I stood against the rush.
It slowed, advanced its tall and
stately waves in a most
sinister silence.
And he was gone.

I didn't know a dream
could be that cold,
its fingers moulding
probing at my bones all day.

The wheel turns.

There's green for birth and spring
in dogwood eye and cedar shoot
and green for death by water.

Unbroken circles loop themselves
tight to the loom's taut warp.
Tension takes time, and
like he used to say, you
can't hurry some things.

Green thread glides from shuttle
feeding from the steady spool.
Weft spins off bobbin
and back in circles
circles . . .

I washed the plain white wool
in a copper tub. The hired
man started on another ewe,
his mouth like weathered rubber
pursed in silent whistling.

In my tranced discipline
I boiled green oak leaves in a bag
with salt and vinegar for mordant,
strained out the leaves and stems.

A clean unfaltering green.
Wordless.

II

Broadway Vision

And in my dream I saw
a man upon a bus on
Broadway at 100th west.
His jaw pure kangaroo, his
nose both wise and black
and bearing spectacles.

Make haste, O God, deliver me
make haste to help, O Lord

No trousers, underpants with
stripes and limp descending
sox. I prayed to wake as
my straphanging neighbour
pressed against me wise
and black upon the bus.

O hurry, Lord, speed to help
your homesick servant

I sought to move, to leave the
brutish bus. In vain. His way
was forward. He moved speedily
as I backslid. And as he
pressed, I pleaded with the
driver in my uprightness:

Oh help me, Lord, to pray
for words are slow to come

Obey my voice, was what I
would have said but tongue
was locked, confounded.
No voice came. Instead, grey
desperate vapours spread
from nostrils, ears and mouth.

O clear the air, dear God,
release my tongue

Besides, the driver wasn't
wearing trousers either.
How can man trust a bus's
destination when no girdle
cleaves the driver's loins?
You cannot and I didn't.

O Lord, make haste
deliver me conventionally

When suddenly a storm smoked
up the windows, towering
clouds blocked out the light
and hail and thunder split
the sky. I strove in silence
with my beast from whose –

O Lord, I can't believe
this bit –

sharp pants were coming
tongues of flame! A trumpet
voice waxed loud in Aramaic:
"Stop the bus! She wants to
leave!" accompanied by balalaika
in the right-hand corner.

O Lord, my swift deliverance?
my help?

Alarmed, the other passengers
divided like the sea. With
faces harder than the rocks
beneath they cursed my *sansculotte*
assailant who then sank
upon his evil kneecaps.

For the day of democratic wrath
is come. And who shall withstand
your communal pressure, O Lord?

Behold, I am standing at the door
of the bus, and am set down at
116th west in Broadway, NYC
safe from tribulation and untrousered
men with spectacles and
heads of kangaroo.

O blessed Lord, you heard my prayer.
From such tight spots have you delivered
me often enough amid the difficulties
between birth and death. But how much
longer will your patience hold?

And as I sang the praises of my saviour
I looked about me in the busy street
and lo, there hurried men with jaws
like kangaroos, with noses wise and
black and bearing spectacles. No
trousers. Underpants with stripes.

I thought I was awake. It seems you
favour those asleep, O Lord.

The women all had pouches on their
bellies, some with young and all
did flee apace with joyful din in
NYC. Only I had neither pouch
nor child. My name was blotted out.
Awake, I longed for home.

I am much afflicted, Lord.
Let me truthfully remember
what it was to be at home.
Quicken me kindly out of
silence to speak the danger
of being too much oneself.

The Call

for Charles Causley's 70th birthday

hello Charles how are ya
mate remember William
Creek I can't talk
long there's other fellers
waiting and a string of
camels kneeling on the edge
of nowhere and a bloody
great phone box stuck in
the sand like a dunny with
everyone wanting to use
it no poetry's nothing like
life not mine anyway if what
I think a poem is a poem
poets are born not made just
like you said but life does
help eh tell them all to drop
dead I'm talking to a poet
yes it's Australia saltbush
sand and spinifex and 45°
in the shade last week not
Cornwall in the winter eh
the South Australian manager
of Telecom told us it will
change our lives a facility
he called it for what that's
worth Bernie's cranky it's not
hotter they'll do just about
anything for a dogfight here
gets chilly on the Simpson
three dogs and a road train
full of horses for the knackers
in Whyalla and a bunch of

paper men photographers the
blokes who put it in and
tourists looking zonked the
manager unveiled the bloody
thing usually only six of us not
much to see and less to do
bit of a treat really otherwise
we wouldn't get to see each other
all that often spotted nearly
sixty all in all here today and
gone tomorrow plus the manager
that young stuffed shirt a
trendy wouldn't touch the amber fluid
wanted wine facility this
facility that me camel's got his
nose in piss off you whiffy bastard
not you old mate I'll write a
proper letter later none of
this microwave stuff with
pips to stop congratulations
anyway there's a strangler in
a cowboy suit bashing down the
door and me camel's dropped
his bundle see ya

Pie in the Sky

for Gwen Harwood

I'm eating an Australian meat pie,
reading a book about
Beethoven's spiritual development.

It's very quiet in Hobart over Easter.
They're all in church.
The pubs are closed.
I've struck it lucky at the deli:
he's Greek.
Life doesn't stop because you're orthodox.

Only connect, said someone bent
on probing creativity's mystery.

I'm only reading casually so –
No excuses, please – a voice bullies me
to order: you're a poet, aren't you?
Try connecting.

And so I do. Try, that is,
twitching the mind's slack elbow.

The pie's distracting, succulent
rich and brown, so unabashed.
It's what it is.

I tell myself no faculty
was every sharpened on a pie,
no complacency every flattened either.

Leave it there.
Let the connections connect without you.
I say this to the one who's eating.

The pie is a synthetic whole,
ripe sonata of crust and meat and crust
baked to rule.

No mice.
No rubber bands.
It's 1989.
Three neat movements, there it stands.
Don't think.
Keep eating.

I pour red sauce to break the synthesis,
tomato scherzo.
Joy to balance melancholy.
The season needs a lift.
Four movements now.

Ordinary experience outwits
your analogues with other arts.

Imagine looking at a painting:
a pie is on a table, nothing more.
Acrylic on canvas, neat as pie,
Hockney maybe.

He'd call it *Pie on a Table*.
If he painted himself eating it
he'd call it *Man Eating a Pie*.

He wouldn't call it *Self-Portrait*, *Nurture* or
The Last Supper which might smack of
egotistical sublimity, claim spiritual
aspiration or a literary humour.
These do not exist.
And if they do, they're only a
projection of our needs.

Needs are for children.
This is adult viewing.

If Andy Warhol took it on
there would be fifty in rows of ten.
50 Meat Pies he'd call it.
Titles aren't the artist's bag.
Still Death would do as well
but never mind — the pudding's
proof enough . . .

It fastens bluntly on your retina,
leaves your spiritual well-being high
and dry, our gold-brown flaky
high-rise pie humped with flocklets
of tomato sauce.
That's art enough.

It's not:

Little Jack Horner's individualistic self-
congratulatory pie,

or the king's hierarchic banquet, beaky
with blackbirds,

or the tragic moussaka of Thyestes
brimming with his children's gristle.

It is:

an Australian pie
legitimate ingredients
approved by Public Health,
no fancy foreign stuff —
we're Fury-friendly here.

Connections are taking care of themselves.
Our juices flow. Steam rises,
ribboning wisps in air.

In music, it wouldn't match
the *Grosse Fuge*, great C sharp,
nor the *Quartet in F* he polished off
at Gneixendorf: "the name sounds like
the breaking of an axletree," he muttered,
inner ear reverberant with connections.

"Muss es sein?
Es muss sein!"
Simple as pie, we say.

What is it then that *is*?
The pie steams open from its crusted skirts,
red gobbets sink below the rim.

If I were marrying music to this pie
I'd tie it to a wheezing barrel organ
from some innocent old carousel.

A crowd is gathering, nodding to
"The Road to Gundagai" and "Come Back to Sorrento".
Round and round the horses roll
their diamond eyes, stiffening
in full stride, biting the air
with wooden teeth,
letting it go at that.

For A.D. Hope

On the occasion of his 80th birthday

Past the open window
a sparrow flies, dips,

shuts its wings, drops
a little, spreads again

to lift   lift
catch itself rising.

Once, nervous, practically
invisible, I dipped into

your sight, pardoned
for whatever it was I wasn't.

Your dreaming head, freckled
delicate as a sparrow's egg,

charted the contours of
a shaky flight.

The lines seemed clear enough,
the hunters far away.

Kindness steadied the uncertain air.

I wrote a poem about you.
An anthologist thought it was about God.
A critical sleuth hinted at an absent father.

Forgiven still, the mind, listening,
catches a feathered rush of memory —

a little air
a clear pane
and a small bird
falling

Growing Up

When I grow up (I'm only fifty-five)
I want to be as mountainous and wise
as Marguerite Yourcenaar.
A big stone sphinx
silent as a shadow.
The perfect balance between
grace and power.

I want to be strong enough to live
on an island off the coast of Maine,
let my beautiful garden run to seed,
receive an interviewer from some
prestigious TV arts programme
once every twenty years, descend
to read aloud with detached hauteur
prophetic passages from past work,
refuse the academy's accolades.

I will not miss my native land.
I'll know who I am.
My voice will be low, steady,
unemphatic, purged of need.
I will not mind being big-boned,
heavy. I will not notice
that my hair is thin,
that my eyes have come to a standstill,
that earnest questions stay unanswered.
The loss of lovers, children's defections
will leave me cold.

I will become the absolute
it's taken me a lifetime to annihilate.

Reading a Letter in Amsterdam

Under chestnut clusters looped in light,
a firm clean-painted bench.
I'm remembering you as you were before
we met, before I sat here with your letter,
waiting, watching children, joggers, lovers
pass, a blurred and broken line.

You've been away a long time
through all our pointless winters.
I've found you now in tenderness
like something lost in childhood,
remembering you as you were before
we met again, before I sat here waiting
on a bench in Amsterdam.

Like distant ghosts, older men and women
slowly pass the bench in silence. I watch unseeing
what's closer to me now than you,
remembering you as you were before,
as you might be now,
before your bright green spring
cut short our winter,
swam us into flower.

Your voice, a longing subterranean stream
has shaped our story, and your words,
those *words*, shake out like rain
in my cupped hands.

You are not with me.
I've come a long way to tell you
this reminds me of some other time,
some other place, but not the same
as what was lost in childhood.

Your letter's shaking in my green-veined hand.
I open it. Not open –
tear is closer to the truth, my hand
still trembling on a firm clean-painted bench
in sun-struck Amsterdam.

The Ballad of the Pretty Young Wife

for Helen Adam

Here is a tale of sorrow and woe
That happened in time so long ago.
An old man nearing the end of his life
Took to his heart a pretty young wife.

A wife to look after his house by the sea
His house forsaken and solitary
By waters dark, perturbed and cold,
The lair of creatures cruel and bold.

Through murky waves the sharks cut light
She heard their path in the dead of night.
She heard them gather, though far away,
And her will moved with them in search of prey.

"Be still, my dear, be still and sleep
Though the waters are dark and the waves run deep.
My little bride, there's no need to dread
The path of the shark in our sheltered bed."

They hunger when only the easterly howls
Those starving sharks with their harrowing jowls
But when old age sags in a sleep profound
The cleaving fins make the only sound.

She dreamt that she swam in the rising wave
Naked and proud and young and brave,
She feared no sound, she scorned the dark,
Pursuing with joy the song of the shark.

Her fettered soul to its own kind sped
As she cleaved the waters dark and dread.
She breasted the waters so cruel and proud
At one with the sharks she sang aloud:

"I'm free at last to seek my good
I lust for my kind and for human food
And I hate the old man near the end of his life
Who welcomed me in as his pretty young wife."

She dreamt next night of a knife-like fin
And the world opened up and took her in,
And she sliced through its waves like her kin, the shark,
And she lashed her tail when the moon turned dark.

"Show me the path on my quest for food.
Show me the source of life-giving blood."
The moon came out from behind a cloud
And shone with force on the old man bowed

In the bed where he treasured the pretty young wife
The source of his joy, the jewel of his life.
She cries to the moon by the waters cold
As she turns in its light from the husband old:

"How can I yield to a husband's will
When the blood runs free and the sharks smell kill?"
But the moon turns dark and the clouds rush past
And the lives of the two are ebbing fast.

The very next night she climbs to bed.
The moon has vanished. She lifts her head.
"Are you coming, my wife, are you coming to sleep?"
"Yes, I'm coming. The stairs are so dark and so steep."

He turns to his wife lying still in the dark
From her blazing blue eye flashes out a hot spark
Like a streak of hell's flame. He lies still as death
As she tosses and turns with her ravenous breath.

She pitches him down as his cries float to sea
"Alas for the monster my bed has set free!"
Tonight she is dreamless. Forever is he,
No longer she'll hunt with the packs of the sea.

For the pretty young wife has discovered her prey
In the arms of an old man who hastened the day
Of his sorrow and woe and the end of his life
When he took in his folly a pretty young wife.

Jacques Tati at the Darwin Hotel

Bonjour, words! Tell me where I am –
A thousand miles from everywhere,
they say.

Palm-fringed patio
a buzz of mauve, cerise,
pink and gold and green,
cascades of luminous bougainvillea,
frangipani fretworking
a weightless turquoise sky.

Mangoes drop their headlong smoothness
down the ropy vines, arched mangrove roots,
tangibles unlimited.

"Minimum dress for this area will be
SHIRTS, SHORTS, SHOES, LONG SOCKS"

The trustful waitress leaves me juggling
tiny plastic rectangles of butter,
marmalade, honey. I ferret clumsily
around the toast.

And there's the coast!

Improbable tall palms
a still metallic sea
and miles of sky.

People going out and coming in.
A boy is sweeping slowly up the path.

Here's a man with sideburns
short and chunky in his long white socks.
Determined.

He's carrying two large cases out.
The path is long, the greenery too frivolous.

And there's his wife. Her back is young and white
but she's not young. She limps to take a frontal shot.
They have to leave.

Her husband makes his second savage trip,
puts down the bags to help her with the light.
The boy is sweeping slowly.

It's hard so far away and she's unsure just where
the metre is. He shows her.
She snaps and snaps again. She's sorry
there's a satyr in the shrubbery
eating toast.

It won't be like the travel posters say.
But after all, a holiday's
a holiday.

Marius in Hobart, 1989

for Rosemary Dobson

Last night I saw an old French film.
A story told in black and white
about a woman's sacrifice for love.

Fanny, the little winkle girl
with shingled hair, gave up her
hope of cosy domesticity,
releasing Marius to his
South Sea island dreams.

It seemed both right and proper
back in Melbourne's old Savoy in the early 50s
before the soul's innocence was ironed out
that men fulfil their dreams
that women wait without hope
that magic sailing ships should come
and go.

Around the gentle pair clucked
hummed and growled a clutch of comic citizens
whose operatic gestures, male worldliness
about premarital sex we used to label
"French".
Always shaping up and backing off.
No broken jaws, smashed skulls
or knives in backs. Only playing at it.
That was our world.

Rejected suitors took it in their stride,
never reached for guns,
got shrunk on couches.

Absurdly waddling Panisse,
a defrocked Alf Garnett with pointed shoes,
enormous bum, retreated graciously,
saw through his folly, growing
out of it, a momentary hero.
We breathed again for Fanny.

The men were fat and comfortable
in cummerbunds and aprons.
Enormous-bosomed women in respectable
black satin, no taint of sin upon its sheen.
All wore funny hats, drank wine at midday,
talking, joking on the generous pavements,
light airs teasing the loosened sails
in a peaceful harbour.

A rakish boater for young Marius,
abortive high-crowned Panama for the provincial
Lyonnais whose weedy moustache, fastidious lips
and twitching nose set him up for ragging.
Presiding over all, benign, absurdly tolerant,
sad-faced Raimu played Césare,
the widowed father.

We all wanted such a parent.
We thought they existed in France.
We believed in the forgiveness of sins.
There seemed to be plenty around.

But Melbourne wasn't Marseilles.
Sinister cranes
crouched over iron-grey warehouse walls.
The streets were empty.
The Savoy wasn't France either.
Other South Sea island tests
have taken place and a ship exploded
somewhere in a peaceful harbour.
Somebody else's.

So when I saw this old French film last night
I couldn't look.
The iron gates have shut.
It's too late to say you want to go back,
too late to say you've forgotten something.
You know you'd be lying.

New Age

There's a man on the radio.
He's being interviewed by a woman
with a thin holy voice.
Her name is Caroline. She's impressed.
The programme's called
"The Search for Meaning".
He's impressed himself.
Between the slabs of self-
improvement vibrate slow harp
pluckings, 30s jazz.
He weaves a hairball round TECHNOLOGY.
She feels improved. Music helps
the ball go down.
"What was it like in gaol?" she breathes.
"Wonderful! It brought the holy monk
out in me!" He's ecstatic.
He tells her (twice) he grew
a beard. Goes on to say the beard
upset the governor of the gaol.
"No man in my gaol has a beard!" he roars
theatrically mimicking the governor's rage.
He has observed himself growing a beard
and found it good.
The interviewer ends her business
with a "Peace Be With You".
You can have him for $12 on cassette
at home.

You never know who's waiting for a spot,
dying to keep you quiet.

Miss Short Instructs Her Latin Class on the Fountains of Nepenthe, 1912

. . . Sparrowhawk
Steiner
Terribile
Titmus and, oh dear,
St Quintin, all here
and unperplexed.

Yes, the guide has just eaten
a raw crab *tremolo agitato*
but never mind; *la volonta di Dio*
and all that. We'll have a drink
soon and yes, Steiner, the rock
is indeed volcanic but the
mount quiescent.

Twelve fountains once,
according to Perelli —
some up high from
inhospitable rocky lips,
others jetting out from
vineyards, orchards
in the middle distance.
The rest near sea and shore.

Ancient healers praised them —
yes, in Latin, Titmus. Maybe
not like science as some
know it but empirical
empirical . . .
Good enough for Galen and
please, Terribile, put away
that frog. Providence supplies
no useless gifts, I know, but
we are not at home, however
evil-smelling. Restrain yourselves.
I know Greece was home to moderation
but is it too much to ask, Sparrowhawk,
that folly not be added to irreverence?

Faced by phenomena that seem
to mock the rational,
be humble, Titmus. Yes, it *is*
the Mediterranean. The guide
is quite all right . . .

Saint Calogero's fountain's what
he said and good for gout,
child-bearing, leprosy and,
if you don't eat lentils,
flatulence. Only sunburn,
Steiner. Your mother ought to
know that leprosy's extinct.
Varicose veins aren't your problem
yet, but ancients had them too.
Scorpion stings and other venomous
beasts — do watch your feet,
Terribile. The snakes are harmless.
I promised that I'd bring
you home alive . . .

The Paradise fountain is
nitrous, Titmus. For distemper.
Farmers fattened up their pigs
and kept them glossy. No,
Sparrowhawk, the Odyssey
took place in Greece. This
happens to be Italy.

Hercules's Fountain proved to
be a laxative, tartaric and
could fix a harelip
vertigo and chilblains,
also a relief from piles the
universally misspelt
haemorrhoids − I see no
contradiction, Titmus.
No, *please*, Titmus, not
just now. I'm sure a little patience . . .

This fountain known as
la Salina, mostly used
by· women for unspecified
complaints. I said
unspecified and meant
it. Recommended also as
a sheep-dip. Let me finish,
Sparrowhawk. The Fountain
of the Virgin − what's so
funny now, St Quintin?

Purgative and blastopeptic,
gave relief from herpes
elephantiasis and
everything of atrabilious
lunatic disposition . . .

Another which we won't pursue
today relieved the Babylonian
itch and other crudities,
fantastic visions, colic,
and affections of the heart
with which some of
you may later be
afflicted. I strongly doubt
that procrastinating
cataplasia was a raging
plague but you may
have something, Steiner.

The guide has told me
of another which, by
virtue of its smell alone
raised from the dead a
certain Anna Pasta lying
in her coffin. It wouldn't
even wake you up,
St Quintin, but try
to look intelligent . . .

The Fountain of Saint Elias
soothes all who suffer
lechery and ingrown
toenails and no, Terribile,
please keep your
shoes on. It was never
dedicated to Priapic rites
no matter what you may
have thought you read.
The text was probably
corrupt . . .

Grazie, the boat *per amore
di Dio*. Why should not a
fountain, Titmus, dry up
if it pleases?

III

Hospice Training

To get there, first you have to pass
the barriers of speech, unlearn
your hard-won plainness.

Is it worth it?

Pass a fence of iron spikes
raised to tear and gut what's crouched behind,
what's dying to get out.

Will it funk the course?
Will it survive?
Will it be free?

Open your eyes.
Try to look as if you're listening.
They're big on empathy here,
dull with concern for the terminally-ill.

I'm feeling murderous,
listening to the air explode
before their words put out the light.

I'm sorry but this is how it is.

When Lucia, Joyce's agonised daughter
heard about her father's death, she said:
"What is he doing under the ground, that idiot?
When will he decide to come out?
He's watching us all the time."

That doesn't sound insane to me.
If you were ever a writer's child
you'd know the terror of a word
from the mouth of a primary carer.

They put her in,
these masters of language,
breakers of the whys and hows of a tale,
deciders of your fitness for the road,
who tell you how to mourn
and how to die.

But concentrate.
Try and forget the words.

Something delicate's alive behind the spikes.
Fix your eye low on that shuddering wing.

It has to be worth it.

Breathing Exercises

Have you ever tried to give your mother breath?

You stand, back to the wall,
a prisoner awaiting execution.

A bad start in life, you might say.
But whose?
We're not talking childbirth.

Desolation keeps you both in check,
as formal as white airless brides.

Her hands undo you, moving in
a slow blind caress,
arching over the clinical sheet
scrunched high in pain.

All you want to do is breathe
the panting mouth alive.
All you want to say, your chances
of being heard saying it,
left the airless room years ago.

Embarrassing scenes in enclosed spaces
were never permitted.

Gagged, you can't move.
Sentence has been passed
without words.

There are no bonds for good behaviour.

Afloat

I knew a father once
who when I said "I want to fly a kite"
became for me a child again,
pretending not to know.

His fingers fumbled with the string
so mine should move more freely,
and everything was airy
blue and light.

In just such ways he taught my arm
a gentle arc in water, laughed me
into dead man's float
and porpoise flip.

Each day I waited for the toy-box
called an Austin
to rumble down the street
between the elms towards a
grey-green Melbourne sea,
jumping the running board
to ride that little strip of freedom
called "our drive" before our mother
collared us to silence:
"Be quiet. Don't disturb your father."

Would it disturb you now
to know I know what duty let you in for?
Or to tell you how, each day,
I wait that day's-end glimpse
of the whispering sea?

Call It Love

They met as prickly children do,
hiding nameless fears.

Their sad ironic faces
promised what they couldn't see.

When he died, she lay awake
an old photo in her head of a boy,
profiled against an apple tree in flower
staring out across the Zürichsee,
infinitely alone.

Curved solid with loss,
his young back shook tears out of her.

All their faltering life she'd hoped
to be a flowering tree for him.

You could call it love.

Reading

NO ALCOHOL: red ink across the page.
Why not, I wonder, hearing again
the social worker's words,
"They've come to die with dignity
so give them what they want."

He's Kavanagh, James Brendan,
steady eyes, fifty-one years old,
a miner from the North, and Irish.
Dependents none.

It's in his lungs.
He sits up straight, alert and shy
his voice smoky as an old song.
"I haven't seen you here before.
You new?"

I've taken Edna's nip next door in 17,
faced Mavis, neck turned tight against the dusk,
who last week chucked her brandy over me
and cried. Both women with no visitors,
children somewhere . . .

"I'm new and so are you.
Your dinner's on the way."
Eve might have greeted Adam so
in God's fine garden, not too bright
as usual, safe on lower ground.

His sheet reads, Cheerful, independent,
likes to talk.
            The room is bare and clean,
no telly and no flowers,
a monkish radio, a phone.
No books.

"D'you read at all?" I ask who never did much else.
"I've never read a book, but I was fit."
"I'll bet you were," I say, thinking of
pitiless Dampier sand and sun that saps
the blood from a green country man,
loading his breath with dust.

His feet are swollen, stretched translucent,
the white V of his thongs still visible
between the sunburnt toes. I touch them gently,
wandering in the blossoming voice of this
mild solitary man. "D'they hurt?"
"No," he says, "just the condition. Nothing."

He knows his shape and substance without dread,
one who came and will go quietly
from this cruel country. My reading falls away.

"But let me tell you about yesterday," he says.
I'm listening, Kavanagh, James, no alcohol.

"They took us to a play, just two of us.
I'd never seen one in my life before,
real people just like you and me!
We heard their squeaking shoes,
the floorboards creak. Word-perfect too,
remembered every line. How do they do it?"

O you, who never read a book
or hatched a child or left a wife,
your mother maybe half a world away,
why ask me that, absurd in Eden?

Unfit, I bend to touch his feet.
My hand shakes and he smiles:
"It's nothing. Really nothing.
Just part of the condition."

Home Care

A rented one-room unit
right above the freeway.
Can you spare four hours tomorrow?
Just the usual — drinks, the toilet, company.
Her husband has to get away
to do some business. There's no one else.
They sold their house in Mandurah
to come to Perth. She's having chemo.
Seventy-five, mastectomy and secondaries.
Doing well, considering. One of our nurses
calls at ten. Her name?
How could I have forgotten —
Constance Bryant.

I've never done a home relief care stint before.
The coordinator's tone is flattering.
I'm scared, but I say yes, slow
to knock back chances these days
to apprehend an ancestor.
Anybody's.
Guilt, I think. I let mine slip away
when I was young and deaf
and indestructible.

Bert her husband's an ex-panel beater,
boyish in his seventies, trying
to keep things tidy. His meek front
speaks of order, devotion and
never a harsh word.
What I imagine might have been
had we been different.

He shows me tea bags, crackers,
half a chicken in the fridge.
Her tin of lemonade.

"Maybe she'll eat a bit of nectarine."
"I won't." Her voice comes strong.
"He's only happy when I eat," she says.

Bert's stooped, pink, hesitant,
a mottled moon-faced innocent,
steel-rimmed specs, a checkered shirt.
I'm softening yet again to fall
for the heroic myth, the Happy Family.

Any children? Two.
A son in the army far away,
a daughter on a farm.
They can't get in.
Dad's looking after Mum.

The freeway hums below the balcony.
I'm watching tiny cars slide by in lines
like metal beetles.
Each one has a driver
going somewhere.

"I've brought a rose for you.
The only one alive from last night's easterly."
Bert takes it gingerly, slowly finds a glass.
There's only one to spare.
"Thanks," she says without her teeth.
Air whistles through the inverted U
of a pugnacious mouth, eyes flickering
back and forth.

He finds it hard to leave
worrying his bulk towards the bed
and back towards the door.

She's propped up looking hard at me.
She misses nothing, taking me back
to when my grandmother lived
and died with us, unschooled.
But sharp.
You couldn't fool her with a rose.

A hard life shaped that jaw
jutting above the sheet, a pale
blue nightie with its girlish trim
against the wasted flesh.
"Just show her where things are
and off you go. Give's a kiss."
He does it all, awkward and slow,
finding the going hard.

"I expect he'll go to the dogs
when I'm gone." She suddenly sits up
after the door clicks shut.
Her eyes have sparkled into witchery.
She laughs, grows larger in the bed.
"You see this table?"
Close beside the bed a little wooden stool
stands painted white.
She strokes the surface lightly.

"My son Gary made it for me.
Just a nipper in the primary he was.
We sold up everything. I kept this.
It's mine. Nobody gets it till I go.
I've left it to my daughter. Would you believe
that when I told *him* that
he suddenly got interested. Never was before.
They'll have to fight it out between them."

Then she laughs again.
"I always wanted something of my own.
I grew up in an orphanage. He made it
just for me. My son did that."

I sit beside the bed
but not too close, slipping
in and out of her mind.
I'm wondering how it feels to lie
inside an empty rented box
touching wood, how it feels
to know you're leaving
what might have been, what may be
or what never was.

She tells me that she's getting by.
"Time for a nap," she says.

A mild wind stirs the curtain.

While she sleeps I'll read the weather
forecast, watch the bushfire's pall
above the freeway.
From that smile about her lips I'd say
she's off and dreaming.
About a homecoming maybe,
or just a small surprise for Agamemnon.

Soup and Jelly

"Feed Fred and sit with him
and mind he doesn't walk about.
He falls. Tell him his ute is safe
back home. Thinks someone's pinched it,
peers around the carpark all the time.
His family brought him in it and
he thinks it's gone.
He was a farmer once . . ."

I take the tray. The ice-cream's almost
melted round the crumbled orange jelly
and the soup's too hot. I know
I'll have to blow on it.

Hunched, trapped behind a tray,
he glances sideways, face as brown
and caverned as the land itself,
long thin lips droop ironic
at the corners, gaunt nose.
The blue and white pyjamas cage
the restless rangy legs.
In and out they go, the feet
in cotton socks feeling for the ground.

"Are you a foreigner?"
"Not exactly. Just a little sunburnt,"
and I put the jelly down. I mustn't feel
a thing: my smile has come unstuck.
I place a paper napkin on his lap. He winces.
"You're a foreigner all right," he says.
"OK," I say. What's one displacement more or less,
wishing I were a hearty flat-faced Fenian
with a perm and nothing doing in the belfry.
Someone like his mother. Or a wife who
spared him the sorrow of himself.

Now he grabs the spoon. "I'll do it."
"Right," I say, "You go ahead. Just ask me
if you want some help." The tone's not right.
I watch the trembling progress of the spoon
for what seems years, paralysed with pity
for his pride.

How does a dark-faced woman give a man called Fred
who cropped a farm and drove a battered ute
a meal of soup and jelly?

Outside the window, clouds are swelling
into growing darkness and there's a man
hard on his knees planting something in the rain.

In Memory, Vincent Buckley
1925–1988

> *Only the dead can be forgiven;*
> *But when I think of that my tongue's a stone.*
>   W.B. Yeats, "A Dialogue of Self and Soul"

Easy to say yes in winter
to a summer hope, the coming of a friend.

Another chance for two cold characters,
lately warmed, to take death's name in vain,
to laugh and maybe sing.
It seemed a simple thing.

Never exactly personal when young
we stood still, going places slow,
harnessed to whispering ancestors.
Catholic and Jew in a dumb and guileless country,
our heavens and hells were never shapeless.

Two solitudes with clever tongues
enough (we thought) to drown
the clamour of the coming night.
Short on small talk, stoned on
art's austere virginities, frozen in our
private dislocations (that's how you might have put it
once) stalking the metal-rimmed rhetoric
that once could turn a simple word like "life"
to something as seditious as "my body's occasions".

We came to call it "life", went on to live it
till our passing's halting breath became
too delicate to name.

You taught me Yeats's hardening into truth,
Joyce's defections. Their Dublin meeting flared
to life in class. Idealist and saboteur,
rootless high-class Protestant and petty bourgeois rebel
struck it rich for us.

Sometimes the body's occasions take on flesh.
Not rhetoric, but knives that slit the heart.
Nothing time's ironic surgery can't fix.

"I tune my muscles for the strait of death," you said,
writing about the Persians in defeat, with maybe
Ireland's mayhem, murder in your mind.
"Life is a history of absences
And unprepared returns," you said.

We don't know who we are when we are,
whisper the ancestors.
Before there's time to blink away your ignorance,
noble language springs the trap shut, earth tips,
and absence stares us back like dull grey stone.
And on that stone is written: there is no return.

We wouldn't dare to start a sentence now with
"Life is" anything
though gaudy Yevgenis of this world keep talking,
change their coats with every wind,
deform their tongues with dogma, answers for the
taking at their fingers' flick.

You said, "Some poets are weathercocks, some
weather forecasters. For myself, I want only
to feel Jerusalem's weather."
Surely a yearning mild enough for God
for all His clamour?

If mortality's a blessing, you are blessed,
leaving the song of yourself, the "holy human"
to stretch us, tail you to the sacred city.

"Innocent, cocky, doomed,
Like a conman" — your words, old mate, loving
the ease, the frankness of American speech,
those blessed morsels of the ordinary,
rarer than ornaments of beaten gold and twice as rare
to those intransigent for truth amid imposture.

Occasions of sin
Occasions of virtue
spin into ribbons of air.

We go. All stays the same.

The timid seed pod of the heart
ripens to bursting in creation's fires.
Nothing time's ironic surgery can't fix.
Except a poem.

The past becomes an island of the dead.
Unready, nearly invisible, I swim around
in shrinking circles.

Like birds of benediction taking flight,
your words describe my path,
wedged in the buoyant wind:

"I walk beside these fires because I must,
In pain and trembling, sometimes thanking God
For what they give me, the few poems
That are the holy spaces of my life."

For Jim
1947–1986

I

The minnow class swims in,
plaids and checks of older, innocent America.
Clear-eyed high jinks simmer to a stop.

These are the eighties. Jim is gone
who once sat sassy-tongued in class
learning the meaning of poems.

I'm in his home, alive.
He's dead in mine.
What's a poem now?
Nobody has a dime left to cry.

There he stood in plaid shirt and Afro,
lanky 26-year-old fresh from Ohio State in Western
Australia.
Hello, heart-string!

Have you practised so long to learn to read?
Have you felt so proud to get at the meaning?
What was all thaddabout? he asked, dying.

Shade stunts a crop, squinches a singer's voice.
I want to jump at the sun, he said.
I want to stretch my lip.
I want to be black, he said.
I'm here.

This was the morning of the day of the beginning.

Heading round the bend in the world,
returning to the loved and limber land he left,
I'm in America.
The minnows in my class today are black and white.

Is it because we love that we leave?
Or travel dust around the doorsteps we were born on?

Remember, he said, remember.

Fear not, be candid, said old Walt.
Dwell a while and pass on.
Be copious, temperate, chaste, magnetic.
But pass.

Jim dwelt a while, passed on, branded by unfamiliar light.
Home lacked the bold sunlight he craved.
Home lacked the bold energy he loved.
What is home? Where is love?

Remember with every leaf his coming.

II

After San Francisco, the pilot crackles out the States:
unfurling Nevada, Utah, Colorado, Oklahoma, passionate
peaks and sierras of the west passing,
passing Little Rock, Memphis, Chattanooga, and Atlanta,
passing over endless grasses, shrouded fields
snapped shut in snow
telling the copious tale of love in magic syllables, natural
as breathing: Okonee, Monongahela, Natchez,
Chattahoochee, Oronoco, Homosassa,
Seminole, Osceola, Econlockhatchee, Tuscawilla,
Moccasin Wallow, Slippery Rock, Apopka,
dropping in night down Florida's wrinkled nose
snorting the Gulf stream, the land charged, infused with
magic names, love's litany.

Did Yirrkala, Djankawu, Ngambek,
Mandogalup, Nyuninga, Kondinin
and Wallumburrawang seed Jim's enchantment too?
Sacred morsels of mystery, crumbs of divinity,
red men and black men stirring in their secret places,
dreaming in our yards.

Copious I break sprigs from the tree of death,
copious the yellow-speared grain rising,
copious the question: why?

God talked to himself in the mountains,
stirred from his platform in his secret place:
Folks ain't ready for souls yet.
De clay ain't dry.

And he sang creation's birth,
how seeds of earth and air, water and fluent fire
fused in empty space,
how gases burned, condensed, the land turned hard,
the seas rushed into place, stones took men's shapes
and all the creatures wandered in the hills.

He sang and laughed.
Death took his first taste,
tender grass being sweetest at dewfall.

III

Jim died, casually brushing by an *Eclogue*
while the catheter burst and merciful
morphine swam his head into silence . . .

> *Like this clay growing hard, this wax melting soft,*
> *In the same fire may Daphnis feel my love's fierce blaze.*
> *For Daphnis I burn.*
> *Let my spells bring him home.*

The minnow class swims in and out.
These are the eighties.
Our feet are set wandering in strange ways.

> *Got on de train didn't have no fare*
> *But I rode some*
> *Yes I rode some.*
> *Got on de train didn't have no fare*
> *Conductor ast me what I'm doing there*
> *But I rode some*
> *Yes, I rode some.*

From Grand Central through the long dark tunnels out
out into highrise sunlight,
out by zigzag fire-escapes spidering the charred and
blackened Bronx,
cratered bombsites, car-hulks black and twisted,
New York's terrible backyard passing,
passing the battered spires, the appalled sky,
passing along the frozen Hudson crossed with strutted steel.
I see two blacks and a dog on the bank.
They pick their way through withered winter grasses,
blackness, wreckage. They stand a moment looking.
Snow clings to rocks at Spuyten Duyvel, Dobbs Ferry,
Ossining, Croton Harmon, the frozen river leading,
leaden sky darkening in patches, in strange cuts and jags

the ice is breaking up, and clapboard houses sink
beside the riverbank, the ranging hills, shadows of hurrying
tides haunting the river's reaches.

The song is passing, covering the earth, your country.
I am in your homeland, you in mine.
We are no longer innocent.

> *Well, he grabbed me by de collar and he led me to the*
>   *door*
> *But I rode some.*
> *Yes I rode some.*
> *Well, he grabbed me by de collar and he led me to the*
>   *door*
> *He rapped me over de head with a forty-four*
> *But I rode some*
> *Yes I rode some . . .*

Staving off old death with song,
Twenty-six years old you came.
Forty thousand years old and more you went,
giving in to chance and change, black boy,
rocked to sleep and slumber,
made and unmade by love.

Who put out the lie, supposed to last forever?
Love is when it is.
No more here? Plenty more down the road.
Take you where I'm going?
Hell no! Let every town furnish its own.
Who cares about no train fare?
The railroad track is there, ain't it?
I can jump at the sun, can't I?
I can ride blind, can't I?
I'm black, ain't I?

Darkness.
The brief and infinitely graceful dance of body,
fluid arc of upraised arms,
the dance in air, in empty spaces,
the rush to bite down,
all, all in beauty.

Remember, he said. Remember.

Black child, I will.
I do.

Notes

page 17   *The body and the soul know how to play*
In that dark world where gods have lost their way.
Theodore Roethke, "The Partner"

page 18   *My pillow won't tell me*
. . .
And it like to die.
Theodore Roethke, "The Apparition"

page 32   Italicised epigraphs to each section of "A Tale of the Great Smokies" are taken from E.V. Rieu's translation of Homer's *Odyssey*.

page 103   *Like this clay growing hard, this wax melting soft,*
. . .
Let my spells bring him home.
This is a rough translation of Virgil's *Eclogue VIII*.

More UQP POETRY

Susan Afterman *Rain*
Bruce Beaver *Charmed Lives*
Gary Catalano *Fresh Linen*
Silvana Gardner *The Devil in Nature*
Rodney Hall *A Soapbox Omnibus*
Rodney Hall *The Most Beautiful World*
Kevin Hart *The Departure*
Evan Jones *Left at the Post*
Peter Kocan *The Other Side of the Fence*
Roger McDonald *Airship*
Roger McDonald *Absence in Strange Countries*
David Malouf *Neighbours in a Thicket*
Philip Mead *This River Is in the South*
Dorothy Porter *Driving Too Fast*
Judith Rodriguez *Water Life*
David Rowbotham *Maydays*
Philip Salom *Barbecue of the Primitives*
Michael Sariban *A Formula for Glass*
John A. Scott *Singles*
Thomas Shapcott *Begin with Walking*
Thomas Shapcott *Shabbytown Calendar*
Thomas Shapcott *Travel Dice*
R.A. Simpson *Poems from Murrumbeena*
Peter Skrzynecki *Immigrant Chronicle*
Bobbi Sykes *Love Poems & Other Revolutionary Actions*
Andrew Taylor *The Invention of Fire*
John Tranter *Under Berlin: New Poems 1988*
Dimitris Tsaloumas *Falcon Drinking*
Dimitris Tsaloumas *The Observatory*
Alan Wearne *New Devil New Parish*
Fay Zwicky *Kaddish & Other Poems*

Selected and Collected volumes:

Charles Buckmaster *Collected Poems*
Michael Dransfield *Collected Poems*
Judith Rodriguez *New and Selected Poems*
Thomas Shapcott *Selected Poems*
Andrew Taylor *Selected Poems*